Francesca

Written by
Vanita Oelschlager

Illustrations by Mike Blanc

Vanita's Dedication

This book is dedicated to my granddaughter Sage
and all my other grandchildren.

Mike's Dedication

For Snail

Acknowledgements

Mike Blanc

Kristin Blackwood

Jennie Levy Smith

Kurt Landefeld

Sheila Tarr

Michael Olin-Hitt

Mrs. Pinkler's name came from Sam, a 5th grader at
Portage Collaborative Montessori School in North Canton, Ohio

Francesca
VanitaBooks, LLC
All rights reserved.
© 2008 VanitaBooks, LLC
No part of this book may be reproduced, stored in retrieval systems, or transmitted in any form or through
methods including electronic photocopying, online download, or any other system now known or hereafter
invented – except by reviewers, who may quote brief passages in a review to be printed in a newspaper
or print or online publication – without express written permission from VanitaBooks, LLC.
Text by Vanita Oelschlager.
Illustrations by Mike Blanc.

Printed in China.
ISBN 978-0-9800162-4-6

www.VanitaBooks.com

Francesca

Written by
Vanita Oelschlager

Illustrations by Mike Blanc

VanitaBooks, LLC

Francesca wants to be grown up.

She thinks about it day and night.

Day and night and night and day

Francesca dreams her life away.

Francesca dreams of being grown

with a career she'd call her own.

If only Francesca knew what to be:

Imagine all the possibilities.

Mrs. Pinkler, who lives next door,

is weeding her flowerbed.

She asks Francesca to please come by

and share the imaginings in her head.

Francesca explains there's so much stuff
she wants to do when she's grown up.
But she's just so tired of waiting
to be big enough.

Mrs. Pinkler chuckles and says,

"Life's a bore without some dreams.

But striving for them all the time

is not as marvelous as it seems."

Francesca knew if she grew up this minute

she could be a rock star

and sing in ways that were really bizarre.

She could die her hair green or purple or pink.

She could wear high heeled shoes and a coat made of mink.

"How, Francesca, can you be a hard rocker

if at first you don't jam in your room,

with the music blaring

and your friends' hair frizzing

holding a microphone made from a broom?"

She might also be a movie star,

and ride through the streets

in a long black car.

She could play a role that strikes a chord,

and win the Best Actress award.

"How, Francesca, will you become a big star

if you don't plan a play in the yard,

have fun and wiggle,

get together with your friends and giggle?"

Francesca knew if she grew up real soon

she'd take the lead role in a famous ballet.

Other dancers would bow as she took center stage.

She would dance on her toes

doing pirouettes as she rose.

"How, Francesca, will you become a prima ballerina,

if you don't twirl around

'til you fall on the ground,

even bump your nose,

before you start wearing tutus and bows?"

Francesca knew if she grew up right now

she could be a great teacher.

She could spread her love of books

to every young creature.

"How, Francesca, will you become a teacher?

To get on the right path,

you first need to read,

to spell and do math."

Francesca knew if she grew up today,

she could run like the wind.

She'd go to the Olympics

and win all the medals,

then be the star in her own TV specials.

"How, Francesca, will you become a gold medal winner,

if you don't run every day

on the beach,

in the sand,

in a barn, in the hay

to the top of the hills,

through the creek and the mud?

You surely, oh, surely

must take a few spills."

Francesca knew if she grew up this minute,

she could become a cheerleader.

She'd have the finest of fine school spirit.

For miles around all would hear it.

"How, Francesca, will you become a cheerleader,

if you don't have to shout at your brother,

do the splits and jump high,

or do cartwheels in the house and annoy your mother?"

Francesca knew if she grew up now

she could be an astronaut.

Up to space she would travel.

All the secrets of the universe she'd unravel.

"How, Francesca, will you become an astronaut

if you don't learn the Milky Way?

You can lie under the stars

on a blanket with your dad

and tell stories of your first flight to Mars."

Francesca knew inside her heart

she'd be a great dog trainer.

She'd teach her dogs to sit and beg

and to do the prized full gainer.

She could teach any dog to be a blood hound

a pedigreed dog or dog from the pound.

"How, Francesca, will you become a dog trainer

if you don't have a dog

to teach the full gainer

to take care of and feed

to know what a dog needs?

If you don't let your mom know you want a puppy,

she may think it better if you just had a guppy."

"Francesca, Francesca, hold on my dear.

You don't want to grow up too fast.

If you become grown up right now,

you can't create your past.

In order to grow up you see,

you must have a long, full history.

You started your life

by being little.

If you go straight to grown up,

you'll miss the whole 'middle.'

The middle is where you go to school,

play games outside and learn the rules.

So hold on little one.

Don't go so fast.

You want your childhood

to last and last."

Your friends are waiting

for you to play.

There's Louis and Mary

and Alice and Ray.

Just stay outside,

and have some fun.

Hop and skip

and jump rope and run.

Francesca don't miss out

on everything in the middle.

There is something magical

about being little.

Vanita Oelschlager

Vanita Oelschlager is a wife, mother, grandmother, former teacher, caregiver, author and poet. She was named "Writer in Residence" for the Literacy Program at The University of Akron in 2007. She is a graduate of Mount Union College, where she is currently a member of the Board of Trustees. The idea for this book came from her granddaughter, Sage. Sage's first picture for the book is included here (*opposite*).

Mike Blanc

Mike Blanc is a life-long professional artist. His artwork has illuminated countless publications for both corporate and public interests, worldwide. For *Francesca*, Mike created the illustrations and the design. He lives with his wife Gail, in sunny Doylestown, Ohio. They enjoy their four children, and five granddaughters.

About the Art

Mike Blanc's illustrations for Francesca began as pencil sketches, which were scanned and stored in digital format for templates and reference. Mike uses computer software to emulate a traditional line and wash method. With the support of a pressure sensitive drawing tablet and desktop computers, he draws the image with a digital "ink pen." Once satisfied with a drawing, color layers are applied with "watercolor" brushes and refined with "blenders." The result shown here, is every bit as expressive as our traditional illustration techniques. Happily, the inkwell never runs dry.

Francesca 12" x 18" graphite on manilla paper. Original concept drawing by Sage.

Creative Play

"This is a beautiful and necessary book, not only for children, but also for parents, child caretakers, and child therapists. In our fast paced world where children are being driven to multiple activities, we don't realize that we are creating Type A personality kids; just "mini versions" of the adults, always looking for the goal ahead, even if it means we are not enjoying today, right now. In this book Ms. Oelschlager reminds us of the loss. We are forgetting the most important part of childhood, which is to PLAY. In the process of having fun during play, children are learning about themselves and their world, their abilities, how to make friends, how to cope with all the ups and downs of their lives. Child Psychologists know that play is a very effective way to reach children and get them to express their fears, joys, anger, and other emotions. Ms. Oelschlager helps us see the point of play in this very FUN book! Otherwise, Francesca could be one of those adults, who achieves her goals and can't understand why she is depressed. I give it a lot of thumbs up!!!"

Dr. Ivonne H. Hobfoll, Child Psychologist

Profits

All profits from this book will be donated to charitable organizations, with a gentle preference towards serving people with my husband's disease – multiple sclerosis.

Vanita Oelschlager